Contents

Crash fabric bangle

Hand woven, dyed silk noil
Image inkjet printed onto Bondaweb and organza

Introduction

In this book I set out to work with materials, which for the most part are easily available. As cost of materials also became a consideration I cast my mind back to my childhood memories and to the austerity of my pre-school days as a "war" baby. I fondly remembered playing with scrapbooks and using flour and water paste to stick my images into such books. As a consequence flour and water paste has been used for quite a lot of the projects in "Textile Adventures".

I have always had a love affair with linen and even weave fabrics and scrim fall into this category for me. The fact that gauze or scrim can be pulled out of shape and manipulated also holds a fascination. People call things by different names and so throughout the book I will refer to gauze as scrim. Whilst experimenting with flour and water paste I started to bond scrim to fabrics and papers - hence my "Scrimmy papers".

Trips to garden centres focused my attention on gardening items such as black weed suppressant and bubble wrap and these have been transformed using mixed media and stitch to create useable items for stitch.

For a long time I have been working with wet baby wipes to colour backgrounds. Baby wipes used instead of a paintbrush give a very different effect. The resulting coloured wipes can be saved and re-used for other projects and in this book I have turned my attention to this.

Fish scales have appeared in my work before but I have never written about them, so as part of my desire to use items which are re-cycled and easily available, I have included them in this book.

Not very often, but now and again, a student who is vegetarian will say that they will not work with silk fibres. These students will now be delighted to hear about so called, "Vegetarian silk". These "vegetarian" fibres are made from cellulose fibres and apart from using them with an embellishing machine you can use them for other exciting purposes as described in this book.

As well as more up to date materials such as Crash fabric, I have had a lot of fun working with cocoon strippings. Cocoon strippings are cheap and easy to work with and as requested by numerous students I have included one of my techniques for working with them to produce book covers and pages that are aged in appearance.

I have been working with pulled pastes for a while but a visit to see the Terracotta Army exhibition sent me in a different direction. I had expected the clay soldiers to be terracotta in colour but was surprised to see wonderful patination, which I attempted to copy in my Chinese warrior vessels. Working with paste for structures as explained in this book is fun and produces easy to work on fabrics.

I have become known for making items that are robust and suitable for purpose and in this book I have continued to work with items such as bags, books, vessels, jewellery and the odd wall hanging.

Inkjet printed scrimmy paper

CHAPTER ONE

Scrimmy Papers, Vessels and Pastes

My "Scrimmy papers", are made by bonding scrim to handmade papers using either a thin solution of flour and water paste or by using a thin solution of CMC powder mixed with water to make a paste.

Many years ago I tried working with CMC paste to create silk papers but I decided early on that I much preferred working with acrylic gloss medium or Jo Sonya's fabric medium to create my silk papers. The CMC paste was therefore left unused for decades. –Not any longer! I now find that using it with scrim is great fun.

CMC paste is like wallpaper paste, without the fungicide. It is in powder form and in order to use it you mix it with cold water to form a paste. All of the paste mixtures used to create scrimmy papers or fabrics in this book were made using a very thin solution. When the pastes dry they leave a matt appearance. Thick paste is not only more costly but also unnecessary and unsightly. The fabulous part about using CMC paste is that it dries clear, is inexpensive, is cellulose based and it does not inhibit the use of devore pastes. Great fun can be had, with very little expense involved.

Other glues such as diluted PVA or sealers such as acrylic wax or Mod Podge can be used to bond the scrim to the paper. Your choice of bonding agent will affect the end result. For example Mod Podge used as a sealer will bond the scrim to the paper and it will be impossible to remove the scrim afterwards. It will also leave a more plasticised appearance. As I wanted to keep costs down I restricted my bonding agent to CMC paste and paste made from flour and water.

When working with flour and water paste You will find that even a thin solution leaves some residue when it is dry. This can, however be a bonus. (Page 14)

The choice of paper will also affect the end result. I worked mainly with kozo papers and lokta papers. Try to select papers that feel tactile and steer clear of writing papers, shiny papers or computer papers.

You can paint, stamp or inkjet print onto "Scrimmy papers" or "scrimmy fabrics".

You can even bond scrim to paste fabric and inkjet print onto that.

Inkjet printed paste fabric with scrim   *Burning logs*

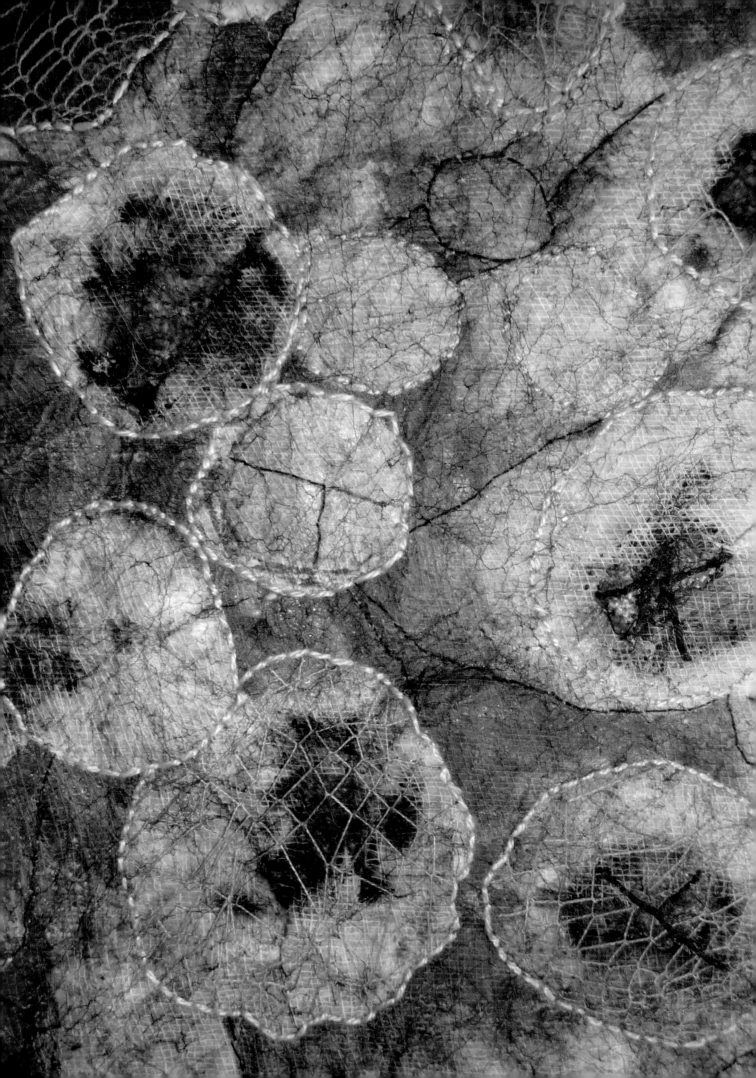

Inkjet Printed Scrimmy Paper Made with CMC Paste

Printing directly onto scrim bonded to paper is straightforward and easy.

1. To laminate the layers it is advisable to work on baking parchment and leave your work to dry on the parchment.

2. I chose to work on textured kozo paper for the base fabric. The paper which I selected had leaves and flowers trapped in it. I turned the paper over so that the back became the front, as I did not want the plant material to be a part of the finished image.

3. Place the scrim over the kozo paper. You could first paint the scrim if desired. I left mine white.

4. Mix CMC paste with water and make a thin solution.

5. Paint this solution over the kozo paper.

6. When it is dry, cut it to A4 printer paper size.

7. Protect the edges by binding them with masking tape.

8. Inkjet print the image onto the scrim covered kozo paper. Your printed image will be matt. I printed sketchbook work onto my sample.

9. Remove the masking tape.

10. Back the work onto a stabiliser prior to stitching. I often use quilter's cotton batting or lightweight Vilene. Try black weed suppressant as a cheaper alternative. I use 505 spray glue to bond the layers.

11. To age your work try painting water over designated areas and scorch the paper with a heat tool. Too much heat may burn holes in the "scrimmy" paper.

Florence

Scrim Bonded to Paste Fabric

Make paste fabric by spreading light moulding paste by Golden on a sheet of baking Teflon or a silicone craft sheet. Use a spatula to do this.

When it is dry, peel it off the craft sheet and work on the smooth, shiny side.

Cut the paste fabric to A4 size and inkjet print onto it. Use CMC paste to bond scrim to the paste fabric as illustrated below. Alternatively embed the scrim in the paste fabric whilst making it. Take care not to push it in too far. (Page 7)

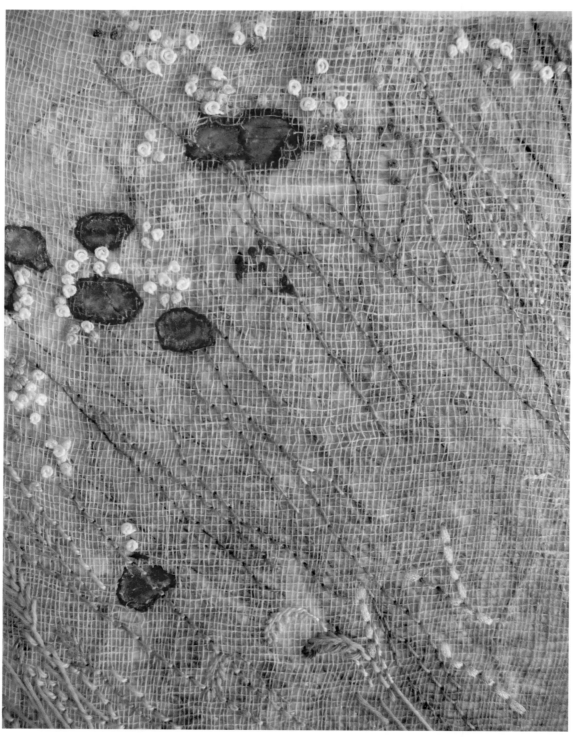

Scrim bonded to inkjet printed paste fabric

Using Scrim as a Resist

Using scrim as a resist works best if used in conjunction with an inkjet printer. The idea is that you will print the coloured design on to the fabric, covered with scrim and then remove the scrim to reveal the white mesh background, which is where the scrim was.

To inkjet print on fabric of your choice, you will need to bond the scrim securely to the fabric or paper. You could use CMC paste as previously described.

1. Place masking tape round the edges and inkjet print the "scrimmy" paper.

2. Decide whether to leave the scrim on or remove it. You will obtain two pieces to work with but both will be paler when they are separated. The scrim will peel off easily.

Try waxing the printed image with clear encaustic wax. It will darken the image.

Scrim removed from the paper

Clear encaustic wax ironed onto the paper

Flour and Water Paste

Paste made from flour and water will leave residue, whereas CMC paste will not. Apart from being a cheaper option the residue left by homemade paste can sometimes be an advantage. (Leopard on the opposite page)

1. Place scrim over paper or fabric of your choice. I used calico for my experiments.
2. Mix flour and water to make a thin paste. Paint this mixture over the scrim.
3. Leave it to dry.
4. Cut it to A4 size.
5. Use a carrier sheet behind it and use masking tape to bond the fabric to the carrier sheet. (My printer will accept this but you may find that you need to iron the calico onto freezer paper.)
6. Inkjet print your design onto the "scrimmy" fabric. (I used Sketchbook work)

7. Remove the masking tape and the carrier sheet. You will have a sharp image.
8. Peel the scrim off. It will have left an impression on the fabric.
9. You can also use the scrim for another project. The image will not be as pronounced. This vessel is made from the inkjet printed scrim, which was removed from the printed calico.

Lutradur 700 is easy to inkjet print on. It is firm and so does not require a carrier sheet. For the examples illustrated opposite, the image of a leopard was printed onto lutradur 700.
Fig 1 shows the inkjet printed scrim on the lutradur.

Fig 2 shows the lutradur, with the scrim removed. Note the patchy appearance you will get using flour paste and scrim as a resist.

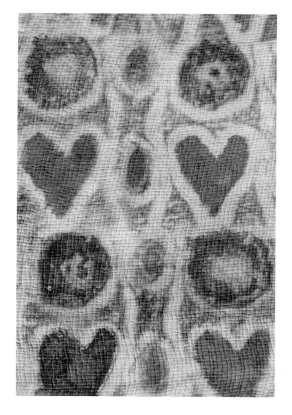

Inkjet printed scrim

Fig 1

Fig 2

Forming Vessels

When designing vessels, which are suitable for stitch, consideration should be given to the type of stitching which will be used, as the interior will be as important as the exterior. Both will be seen and in order to execute the stitching you must be able to insert your hand into the well of the vessel.

A Japanese style teacup, without handles was used as the mould for many of my vessels.

Re-use plastic food bags to form a barrier. Ensure that they are clean. They can be placed over vessels to form protection for the mould. It is important that the plastic bag can be pulled tight and tucked into the well of the vessel. It is there to form a barrier and needs to be skin-tight.

Substituting cling wrap works in some instances but not all. For example, if you use cling film and light moulding paste the film will adhere permanently to the vessel. Baking parchment is a better alternative in this instance.

Search for interesting shapes to use as a mould. One of my favourites is a plastic bowl, which was sold with a Christmas pudding inside. Re-using things, which were sold for a different purpose, can save lots of money and can be an essential part of the design.

Rubber bands, which are often found round vegetables in Supermarkets, can hold things in place and clothes pegs placed around the rim will make life easier when forming vessels.

Hydrangea vessel
Scrimmy paper, dried hydrangea petals
Crackle paint

"Lost treasure"

Rigid vessels that can be stitched into are the main focus on the following pages. The rims can be uneven or more formal.

To age the rims on the vessels illustrated here Szerkezet fabric has been used. Szerkezet is a grey fabric that can be distressed and painted.

The vessel "Lost treasure", is made from thin bought handmade paper, light moulding paste and scrim. It also has embossed copper shim round the top of the vessel.

Henry's vessel illustrated below has szerkezet round the rim. This vessel has been embroidered outside and inside.

To embroider the inside of vessels you should turn the vessel inside out, execute the embroidery and then turn it back again. All of the vessels are robust and you will find that you are able to turn all of them inside out if required.

Henry's vessel illustrated below represents the Field of cloth of gold and also the dissolution of the monasteries. The rim represents the lead, which was stripped from the roofs. The stitching inside the vessel represents ruche sleeves, which were fashionable in the time of Henry VIII. The vessel is made from scrim, paper and light moulding paste.

Henry's vessel

Vessels with Folds

Begin by making the scrimmy paper. Work like this:

1. Select a basin or vessel to use as your mould. Japanese style teacups without handles were used to make these vessels. Begin by placing the vessel in a plastic bag and tuck the excess into the well. (Fig 1)
2. Decide whether you want the scrim to be on the outside or inside. Place the vessel in the centre of your "scrimmy" paper.
3. Turn one of the edges up and bend it over the rim. Hold it in position with a peg.
4. Turn the opposite side up and bend that in position over the rim. Hold that in place with a peg.
5. Gradually turn the fabric over the rim and work out where the creases will go. Remove pegs and reposition them until you are satisfied with the arrangement. Continue round, forming pleats as you go. (Fig 2)
6. All of the "scrimmy" paper should be wrapped round the vessel and tucked inside.
7. Use a paintbrush to paint the base and bottom area of the vessel with a thin solution of CMC paste. Gradually work up the sides and remove one peg at a time and paint that area with the paste.
8. When all of the pegs have been removed check that all of the gauze covered paper has been painted with the glue. Caress the vessel to smooth out any imperfections.
9. Leave it to dry on baking parchment.
10. When it is thoroughly dry it can be removed. Begin by pulling the plastic bag out of the well.
11. Then turn the plastic bag and residue paper down over the vessel.
12. Gently run your thumb under the inside rim to ease the plastic off the vessel.
13. Pull the plastic and the paper and the newly formed vessel will be released.
14. Remove the plastic bag.
15. Use scissors to cut away the excess paper. (Fig 3)

Fig 1

Fig 2

Dried petals, flock or cocos fibres are just some of the things that you can go on to add. (Page 20. Fig 1, Fig 2, Fig 3.)

Instead of wrapping scrimmy paper round the mould try tearing rectangular strips of paper, cut the scrim in irregular shaped pieces and laminate them so that they overlap on a plastic covered mould. Use CMC paste to laminate the layers. (Fig 3 on page 20)

Fig 3

Stretchy Fabrics

Try experimenting with fabrics that will stretch. You will find that you can cover vessels without any folds forming. You will need to manipulate the fabric in order to make it stretch and this will cause some distortion.

Scrim works well for this technique, as does vegetarian silk. Vegetarian silk is described in greater detail on page 37.

SCRIM

1. Because scrim is thin it wraps easily round a mould. Protect the mould with a plastic bag and then try wrapping the scrim round your vessel. Tuck all of the ends in the well. (Fig 1)
2. Use it on its own for lightweight vessels or combine it with other materials. (Fig 2 on page 20)
3. Paint CMC paste over the layers and leave it to dry.
4. When it is dry, remove it from the mould and trim the edges if desired.

VEGETARIAN SILK

a) These cellulose fibres can be pulled and distorted. They wrap round a plastic covered mould without forming pleats and creases. Tuck the ends into the well. (Fig 2)
b) Cover with CMC paste and leave it to dry.
c) When it is dry remove it from the mould and trim the rim. (Fig 3.)
d) If the vessel is sealed with gloss Mod Podge sealer it will look very different. The sealer darkens the colour. (Fig 6 on page 20.)

Fig 1

Fig 2

Fig 3

Working with Scrimmy Papers

Thin papers made from kozo paper or lokta papers that are laminated with scrim can make super little vessels. Paper and scrim, used together will be a little bulky and you will inevitably have folds and creases in certain areas. You can go on to incorporate these creases in your design.

The stitching used on the vessels illustrated in fig 1 and fig 2 centres round the fold lines created on the vessels whilst forming them on the mould.

Begin by making the scrimmy paper. Use pegs to hold the scrimmy paper in position over the mould. Proceed as explained on the previous pages.

Fig 2

Fig 1

The stitching of the heart motif on the vessel illustrated above also follows the fold lines created as it was formed on the mould.

Vessels made in this way will be light but appealing.

They make fabulous containers for special occasions such as weddings and of course they can be personalised with the embroidery.

BEADED VESSELS

Scrimmy paper, made with scrim and thin papers such as raindrop papers make exceedingly light, tactile vessels. If they are to be beaded then they look best if they are beaded inside and out.

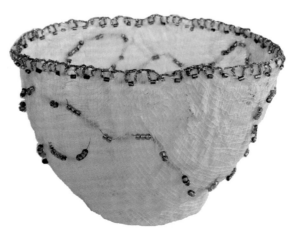

Fig 3

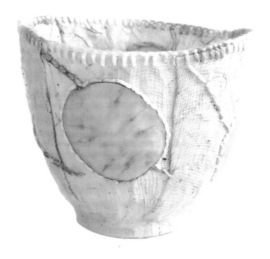

Fig 1: Honesty petals with scrimmy paper

Fig 2: Scrim, flock, cocos fibres

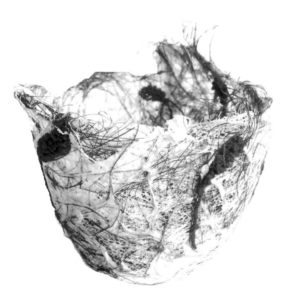

Fig 3: Scrim, paper, cocos fibres

Fig 4: Vegetarian silk

Fig 5: Vegetarian silk, scrim

Fig 6: Vegetarian silk sealed with Mod Podge

Jacket on Scrimmy Paper

Using scrimmy paper as a base for a vessel and then dressing it is fun. The "jacket" should become an integral part of the vessel. My vessel illustrated below represents tangled undergrowth.

1. I began by making scrimmy paper, with red cocos fibres trapped in it. This was used to form a vessel over a mould.
2. The jacket was crocheted in green raffia. This was then pulled over the scrimmy paper vessel.
3. The vessel and the "jacket" were placed back over the plastic covered mould. "Toad Hall" PaperArtsy Fresco paint was painted liberally over the outside of the vessel.
4. When it was dry the vessel was removed. Because it was so heavily painted, the green paint seeped through the holes in the "jacket" and partially coloured the inside of the vessel.
5. The vessel was embroidered with dyed twine.

"Tangled Undergrowth"

Cocos Fibres

Cocos fibres are harvested from the husk of coconuts. They can be bought in bundles that are bleached. They can be used as they are or they can be coloured before or after application.

I used them in conjunction with thin bought raindrop paper and scrim.
Instead of working with large sheets of fabric to wrap round the mould try cutting or tearing irregular shapes to laminate them to the mould.

1. Cover the mould with a thin plastic bag and tuck the excess into the well.
2. Mix a thin solution of CMC paste.
3. Tear natural coloured paper and dyed cocos fibres. Cut the scrim into irregular shaped pieces and distress the edges. Bond the layers of paper, scrim and cocos fibres to the mould.
4. Apply them by overlapping them in different directions and covering them with the CMC paste.

"Prickly pear"

Light Moulding Paste

There are many ways in which to work with Golden light moulding paste fabric, some of which I have covered in previous publications. The "paste" fabric is both strong and durable. It can however leave marks on wooden furniture and so the base should be covered with another fabric if it is to stand directly on furniture.

SINAMAY

Sinamay is that fabulous fabric used by milliners to create wonderful hats. It works by simply wetting it with water and leaving it to dry over the required shape. I re-used a Christmas pudding basin to create my vessels, which are made from sinamay and light moulding paste.

How I worked:

1. Cut the Sinamay to size and place it over the upturned bowl. It looks best if you leave the Sinamay proud of the bowl and do not cut it flush.
2. Secure the Sinamay in place by pulling an elastic band over the bowl.
3. Hold the elastic band in place by securing it with clothes pegs.
4. Pour cold water over the Sinamay. Ensure that it is all wet and then leave it to dry.
5. When it is dry it can be removed and it will have taken on the shape of the bowl.
6. Cover the same bowl with baking parchment. (Note that some plastics will be permanently adhered if you use these instead.)
7. Place the pre-formed Sinamay over the bowl.
8. Use a spatula to apply the light moulding paste. You want to try to get it as smooth as possible and also retain some of the texture of the Sinamay.
9. Leave it to dry. Use the elastic band and pegs to secure it if necessary.

"Seashore"
Sinamay. light moulding paste, puff paint

Mirror Images

Pelicans
Sinamay, light moulding paste

If you want to have mirror images on your vessel you could work like this:

1. Draw your design on the outside of the vessel.
2. Outline it in Running stitch or Backstitch or Stab stitch.
3. Paint the images on the outside. When these are dry you can then paint the images on the inside. You will easily know where to paint, as the stitches used to outline the images will act as your guide.
4. Paint the background, inside and out.

Sinamay and light moulding paste make up the layers of the pelican vessel. The base has been covered with fabric so that the moulding paste will not damage the furniture it rests on. For the seashore vessel opposite this was not necessary as the sinamay forms the base.

"Fish in the net", illustrated below is made from vegetarian silk. The vessel is rigid because the inside has been sealed with Mod Podge so that it is waterproof.

Silver fish on the inside mirror the fish on the outside. The silver and the blue fishes were painted in wax using an encaustic stylus.

Fish in the net

Light Moulding Paste

TERRACOTTA ARMY

Structures that can be stitched into can be made with the help of home made pastes, bought fibre pastes or moulding pastes. Light moulding paste is expensive but it does leave an appealing finish and it is easy to stitch into. This was the medium that I selected to use for my vessels based on the Terracotta army. The Generals bow is depicted opposite and is made from twisted sinamay and light moulding paste.

Sketches were used to simplify designs on the warriors breast armour. The decoration on their uniform is represented in these pieces.

General's bow

How I worked:

1. For the base fabric I wanted something that would be strong and rigid but at the same time supple. I also wanted something that had holes in it so that paste could be pushed through the holes. I experimented with mosquito netting and pulp papers but in the end settled on woven paper matting. (Fig 1)

2. Not having baking parchment to hand an empty cellophane cereal packet proved to be "just the job" to act as a substitute for baking parchment.

3. The woven paper was placed on the empty packet and a spatula was used to spread and push the paste through the holes. This was an essential part of the design, as I wanted bobbles of paste to appear on the surface.

4. It was left to dry and when it was later removed the tiny beads remaining on the paper were retained for further use.

5. The woven paper was painted to represent the patination on the clay figures.

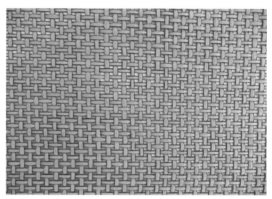

Fig 1

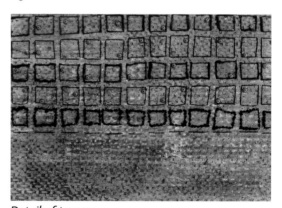

Detail of towers

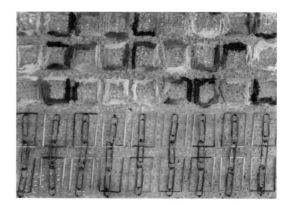

Mosaic Tiles

Using left over moulding paste fabric to create tiles for mosaics is time consuming but good fun. Light moulding paste fabric is easy to make and brilliant to stitch into. In this section I explore some different techniques for working with this ancient art form.

Moulding paste fabric is made by spreading light moulding paste on a silicone craft or Teflon baking sheet and leaving it to dry. The resulting "fabric "can be used for many applications.

Working with stamps:

1. Use scissors to cut small tiles out of the paste fabric. This is a good way in which to use up off cuts of the fabric. They look best if they are not all regular in shape.
2. Identify your design source. Trace it onto tracing paper. A simple design works best. My design for the stamp measures 24cmx13cms.
3. Transfer the design onto a thin piece of Funky Foam (The colour does not matter.)
4. Cut out the design.
5. Use PVA to bond your new stamp to a block of wood. (Fig 1)

Fig 1

6. Use an inkpad to stamp the design onto lightweight Vilene or pelmet Vilene. Use the same stamp to print the design onto teabag paper or bookbinders tissue.

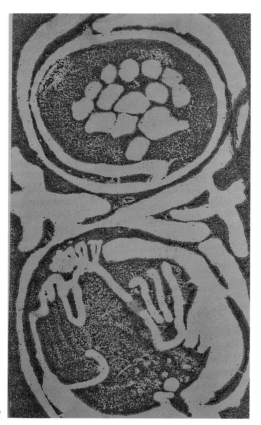

Fig 2

7. Arrange the cut out tiles on the Vilene. Follow any curves. (Note- placing them in a regular grid formation does not work well.) When you have worked out the positions they can be bonded to the Vilene. I found that I prefer to bond them using 505 repositionable spray glue. This momentarily keeps them in place, is easy to stitch into and makes it easy to re-arrange them if necessary.
8.   When the design has been filled with the tiles the background should then be filled in with the rest of the tiles.
9.   Place the stamped teabag paper image over the tiles. If you are happy with the composition use Mod Podge to paint over the paper. As the paper is porous it will seep through and as it dries the paper will be bonded to the tiles.
10.   You can now stitch into the design. (Yorkshire rose - opposite page.)

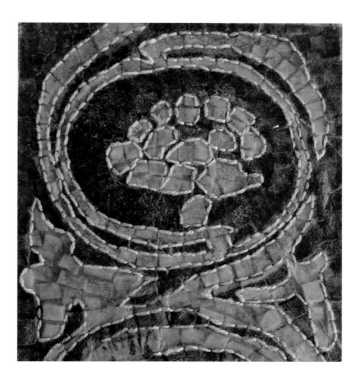

Yorkshire rose

Left over moulding paste fabric can also be used to make punched circles. The resulting beads can be used for surface decoration or for dotty mosaics.

1. Use a hole punch to make lots of light moulding paste circles out of paste fabric.
2. When you have sufficient for your design use 505 spray glue to bond them in position on lightweight craft Vilene or pelmet Vilene. (For the thistle image the holes were placed in a grid formation.)
3. Inkjet print your image onto thin paper (Fig 1) or light see through fabric (Fig 2).
4. Place it over the punched holes. Laminate it with Mod Podge. (Fig 1) Or simply stitch into the layers. (Fig2)
5. Stitch into it.

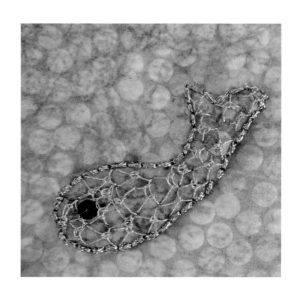

Fig 1

Fig 2

Pulled Paste Fabric

There are many applications for pulled paste fabrics. You can pull the paste itself as described below, or you can pull paste layered on other fabrics or papers.

You could work like this:

1. Use a spatula to spread a generous layer of light moulding paste on one silicone craft sheet or Teflon baking sheet.
2. Place the second sheet of silicone on top.
3. Use the flat palms of your hands to spread and squash the paste.
4. Lift one corner of the silicone sheet and hold the layers down with your other hand. Gently pull the top layer off. It will pull the paste and distort it.
5. You will have two sheets of silicone craft sheets with textured paste on them. If you like what you see, leave them to dry. If not, then take the spatula and scrape it off, return it to the jar and start again.
6. When it is dry you can remove it and colour it with paints of your choice. (The raised surface can be used for rubbings when it is thoroughly dry.)

Try:

a. Trapping scrim in the layers or adding dyed scrim as a covering as illustrated in the red tower.
b. Try working on top of textured surfaces such as mosquito netting or woven paper.
c. Try working on textured, waxed papers, illustrated opposite –bottom right.

Pulled paste tower

Pulled paste box

Detail of coloured pulled paste

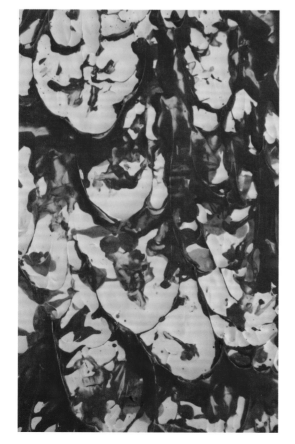

Detail of pulled paste, partially painted

Detail of coloured pulled paste with textured paper

CHAPTER TWO

Heat Distressable Tissue

Opaque heat distressable tissue has limited use for wearable art but it can be used for vessels and wall art.

I prefer to layer it up with other fabrics.
The vessel, "Undergrowth", consists of scrimmy paper, dyed cocos fibres and heat distressable paper, layered in that order. The paper is distressed with a heat tool. Cocos fibres are made from the husk of coconuts and are flammable. Care should be taken to ensure that you do not burn the layers.
Always wear a mask and do not breathe in any fumes.

"Burning logs", illustrated on page 8 is made from black weed suppressant, cotton batting, heat distressable tissue, scrimmy paper and dyed cocos fibres. Devore paste was applied in the centre of the logs. When these layers were burnt back with the heat tool, I worked over a sink and wore a respirator. The centre of the logs did actually burn and each patch was doused under cold water before it could ignite properly. The weed suppressant was added after "the burning".

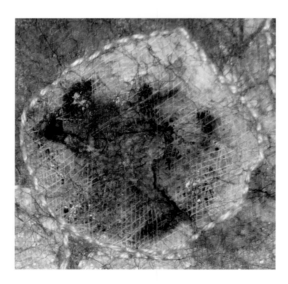

"Wet rocks", illustrated opposite consists of scrimmy paper with dyed cocos fibres and the heat distressable tissue on top. The heat distressable tissue was bonded using CMC paste. The final colour was applied using Tim Holtz alcohol inks.

"Poppies", illustrated opposite is made from red even weave linen, heat distressable tissue and dyed scrim.

"Wet rocks"

"Poppies"

Devore Paste

Devore paste and Fiber Etch are pastes, which are used to remove fibres in selected areas. These pastes work on linen, cotton, rayon and cellulose fibres.

If CMC Paste is used to bond cotton scrim to thin papers then Fibre Etch or other Devore pastes can be used to distress both the scrim and the paper. CMC paste is cellulose based and will not inhibit the use of Devore pastes and as such it is a good glue to use to bond scrim to papers or fabrics that are to be further distressed with Devore paste.

Experiments should first be made to ensure that the pastes do what you want them to do on your chosen fabric or paper.

You will need:

- Thin paper
- Scrim
- Devore paste or Fiber Etch
- Heat gun
- Black weed suppressant
- Cotton batting (Optional)
- 505 repositionable spray glue
- Sewing thread

Suggestions for working;

1. If you want to distress both the scrim and the paper, first test the paper to see if it will distress with the Fibre Etch.
2. Bond the scrim to the paper, using a thin solution of CMC paste.
3. When it is dry, use a nozzle to squeeze a thin layer of Fiber Etch onto the scrim working the design of your choice. If you are not confident to sketch with the paste directly onto the scrim and paper then you could use traditional methods of tracing your design onto tracing paper and transferring it onto the scrim paper before squeezing the glue in the designated areas.
4. Use the heat from an iron or heat gun to dry the paste. It should turn brown.
5. If you want to caramelise the colour on the paper then prolonged use of the heat gun will do this.
6. To remove the paper and scrim from the selected areas wear a mask and work outside. Use the sharp end of scissors or the blade from a scalpel to scrape where the brown Devore paste has been. It will disintegrate.
7. Layer the fabrics in this order-cotton batting, weed suppressant and then the scrimmy paper. Weed suppressant obtainable from garden centres is cheap to use as a stabiliser. It is also useful if you want a black background. I use 505 repositionable spray glue to bond the layers of fabric. (Cotton batting is only necessary if you want a quilted effect.)
8. Stitch into the layers.

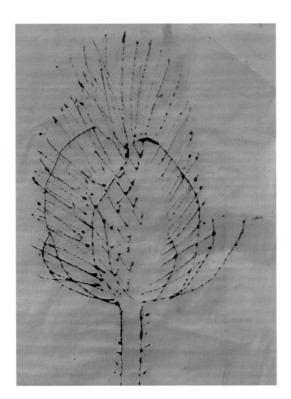

"Seed heads"

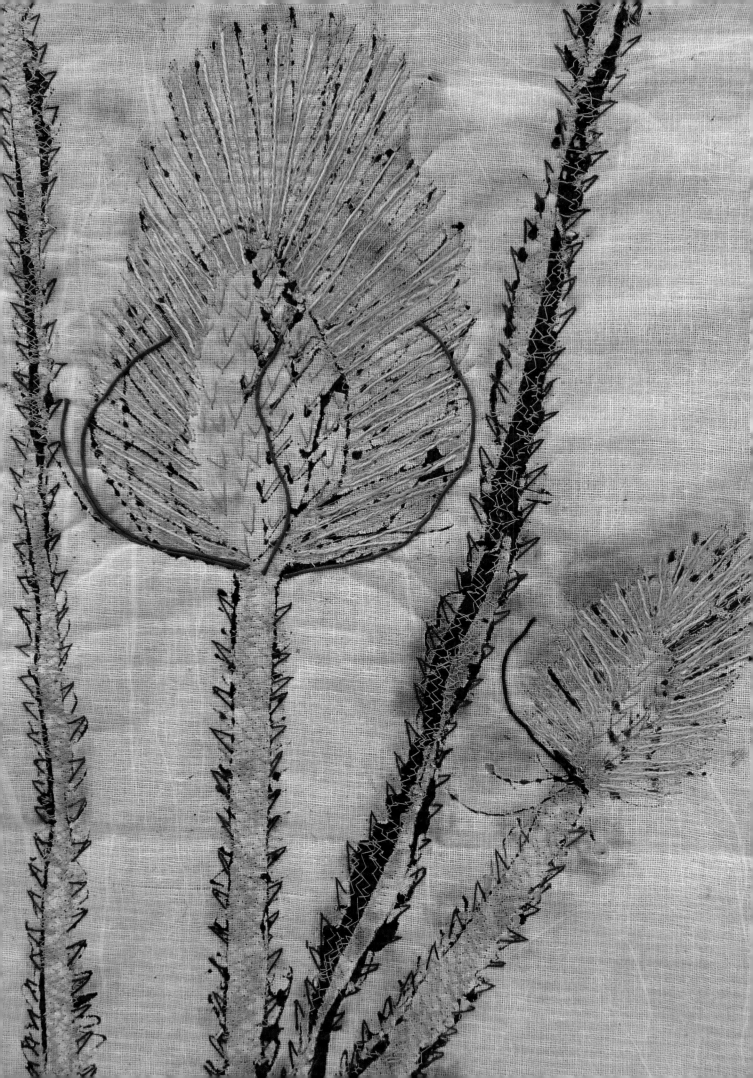

Multiple Layers

Multiple layers of mixed media were used to create the image illustrated opposite and the bangle below. You can work on the paper of your choice. These were worked on an A3 sheet of lokta handmade paper from Nepal. This paper is sometimes called Khadi paper. I worked with the thin variety. 20-40gsm

You will need:

- Heavy duty Pelform Vilene
- Black weed suppressant
- A3 sheet lokta 20-40gms
- Light moulding paste
- Stencil and spatula (optional)
- Scrim
- CMC paste
- Fiber Etch or Devore paste
- Paints of your choice
- Baby wipes
- Clear encaustic wax
- Clear beeswax polish (optional)
- Machine sewing threads

Method:

1. Use the stencil, spatula and light moulding paste to transfer your design onto the light lokta paper. (I did not want my design to be too bold so I used the paste sparingly.)
2. When it is dry place scrim over the top. Bond it to the paper by painting a thin solution of CMC paste over it.
3. When this is dry use Fiber Etch or Devore paste sparingly to outline sections of the design. Do not be too precise.
4. Use a heat gun to activate the paste but do not scorch the fabric.
5. Leave overnight and then lightly brush the paper to remove the excess disintegrated scrim. (Do this outside and wear a mask.)
6. Use an encaustic iron or a flat iron set on low to iron clear encaustic wax over the paper. It will soak right through to the other side.
7. Use water based spray paints to colour the fabric. I used Adirondack spray paints.
8. When it is almost dry use baby wipes to knock it back and remove some of the colour. (Keep the baby wipes for another project.)
9. Layer the Pelform Vilene on the bottom, then the black weed suppressant and then the kozo paper. Stitch round the outside edges to hold them in place.
10. Use free machine embroidery to decorate the paper,
11. Use paper towels to apply and buff clear beeswax polish into the paper. (Initially it will soak into the fabrics and make it look dull. Elbow grease is needed to bring out a bloom.)

Multiple layers used to create the fabric for the bangle

Vegetarian Silk and Devore Paste

This "Tatty rose chic" fabric was made by layering silk paper, dyed scrim and vegetarian silk. Because vegetarian silk is composed of cellulose fibres devore pastes such as Fiber Etch can be used to distress it. Silk paper, made with acrylic gloss medium cannot be distressed with Fiber Etch and so it makes a robust base fabric for the bag.

Work like this:

1. To make the silk paper, protect the work surface with plastic. Spread dressmakers net on this. Tease and pull the silk fibres out. Place them on the net and layer them up in different directions so that there are no gaps. Cover with a second layer of net. Wet the fibres. Mix one teaspoon of acrylic gloss medium with four teaspoons of water. Paint this over the sandwiched layers. Use the flat palms of your hands to push the medium into the fibres. Turn the layers over and repeat. Hang the dripping layers up to dry outside. When they are dry the net can be removed, and the silk paper ironed.

2. Cover the silk paper with dyed scrim.

3. Place vegetarian silk on top.

4. Stitch diagonal lines into the layered fabrics.

5. Use Fiber Etch or Devore paste in designated areas. I used it in each square.

6. When it is dry use the heat of an iron or a heat gun to turn the paste brown. If using an iron cover the work with baking parchment. Work in a well-ventilated area. Care should be taken to ensure that you do not scorch the fabrics.

7. Run the fabric under cold water. This will remove the excess vegetarian silk in your designated areas.

8. Leave the fabric to dry.

9. Hand stitch over the tramlines.

10. If you want to stabilise the remaining vegetarian silk you should consider using a needle punching embellishing machine or a hand needle-punching tool.

11. Look out for needles with large eyes so that you can sew with bulky yarns and wools. I use leather or upholstery needles.

Tatty rose chic bag

Detail of "Tatty rose chic"

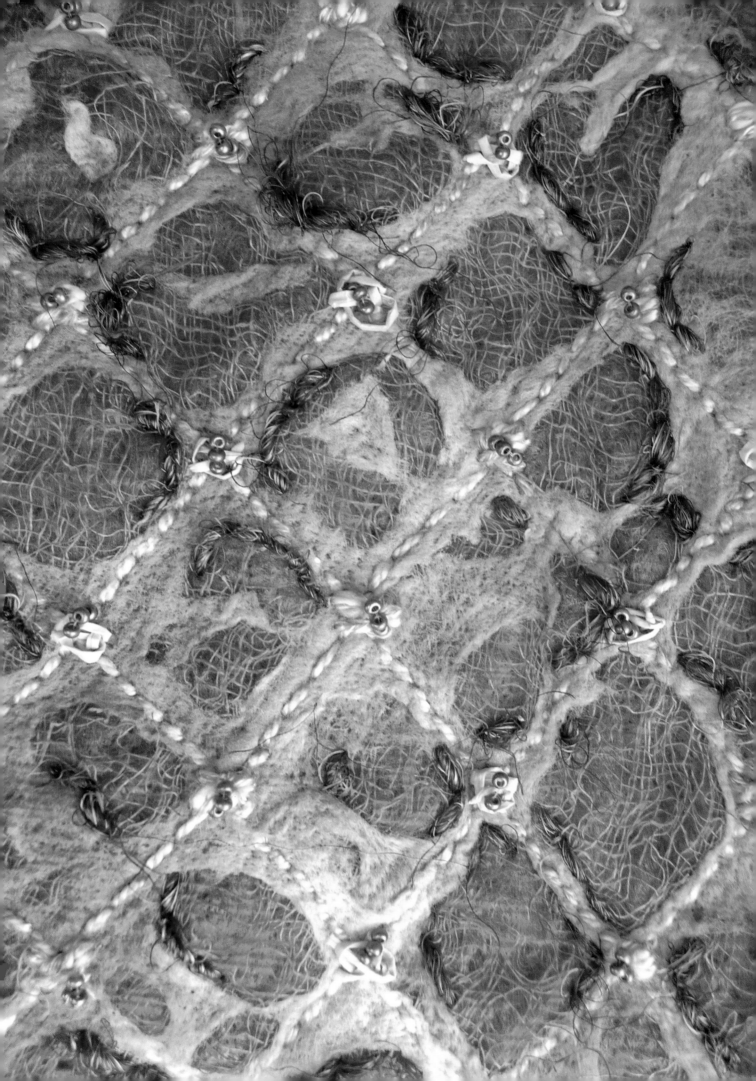

Texture Magic and Vegetarian Silk

Texture Magic looks like shiny cheap dress lining fabric. The intention is that you will place another fabric on top and stitch into the layers. Distortion is created by shrinking the fabric using the steam from an iron.

Work like this.

1. Colour cotton fabric with dyes or paints of your choice. As it will all eventually be sealed with Mod Podge it does not matter which colouring agent you use. (Adirondack spray paints used here. Fig 1)

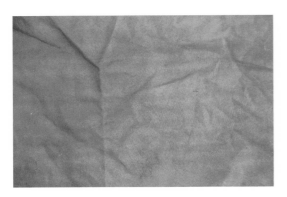

Fig 1

2. When it is dry place the fabric over Texture Magic.
3. Machine stitch into the layers.
4. Hold a steam iron over the Texture Magic. Do not touch the fabric with the iron. It will distort by up to 30%. As it distorts it will pull the cotton fabric with it.
5. Add colour or highlights as desired. (Gold used here.)
6. Paint Mod Podge sealer over the puckered fabric. (Fig 2)

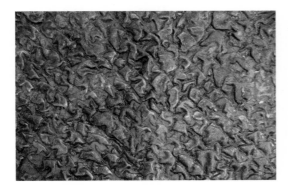

Fig 2

7. Place vegetarian silk over the fabric.
8. Sew diagonal tramlines on the layers. (Fig 3)

Fig 3

9. Use Devore paste in designated areas. Activate it by heating it with an iron or heat tool as previously described.
10. Run the fabric under cold water. The excess vegetarian silk will be removed.
11. Hand stitch or couch over the tramlines again.

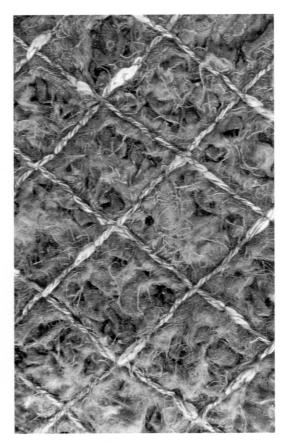

Texture Magic and vegetarian silk

Smocking Thread and Vegetarian Silk

Rather than use Texture Magic to shrink fabrics you could try Smocking thread, made by Madeira. This thread shrinks when steam from an iron is held over it.

1. Begin by stitching into the fabric or layers of fabric. (Habatoi silk and Crash fabric used here.)
2. Shrink the fabric by holding a steam iron over the surface. Do not iron the fabric. Distortion will occur as the thread shrinks with the steam from the iron.
3. Dye the fabric. I used silk dye. Wet the fabric with water and then either paint the dye on or submerge the fabric in a dye vat.
4. Cover with vegetarian silk and work as described on the opposite page.
5. I used fishing wire coloured with alcohol ink to loosely embroider sorbello stitch knots in the spaces.

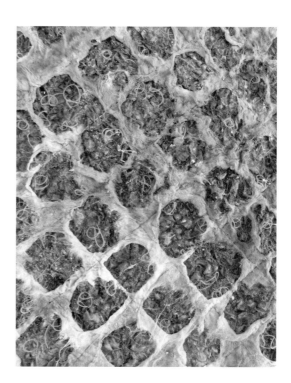

Crackle Paints

Over the years I have had an ongoing love affair with crackle paints. Each make does a different thing and they are all appealing. When a new one comes on the scene I cannot resist trying it out. My main, over riding concern is that the crackle paints or pastes should be fit for purpose and as I mainly make items that are to be used I need to ensure that the crackle paint will stay in place when it is stitched into.

For the sketchbook work illustrated below, I used two different crackle paints. The image of the fossilised creature is coloured with Tim Holtz crackle paint, a medium that I have talked about in previous publications.

The background has been crazed using transparent Croco on top of other paints.

Tim Holtz distress crackle paint and Transparent Croco

PaperArtsy Fresco finish and Crackle glaze on lutradur 700

Paperartsy Fresco Finish and Crackle Glaze

I have really been enjoying working with these paints. They are chalk acrylics. The chalk acrylic paint does look matt. I used it to colour the raffia and paper on the "Undergrowth" vessel on page 21.

The crackle paint, which can be bought to accompany these paints, works by cracking the paint underneath.

Work like this:

1. Paint one of the Fresco finish paints from PaperArtsy in the area to be cracked.
2. Wait for it to dry.
3. Paint the clear crackle glaze over the acrylic paint. Wait for it to dry or speed it up using a heat tool.
4. Paint a third layer of Fresco finish paint over the area to be cracked. It will start to crack before your eyes.

Close up of PaperArtsy crackle paint

Medieval tiles
Moulding paste fabric appliquéd to textured kozo paper

44

Crash

Crash fabric is made by Vilene. It is a man made see through crinkled fabric. You can tear it, burn it, and layer it up on other fabrics. Here are some suggestions for working with it.

You will need:

- Bondaweb fusible webbing
- 2 pieces of Crash, the same size as the webbing
- Baking parchment
- Iron

Method

1. Cut a piece of Bondaweb to the required finished size.
2. Cut two pieces of Crash the same size as the Bondaweb.
3. Place baking parchment on the ironing board.
4. Place one piece of Crash on the baking parchment.
5. Cover it with Bondaweb with the glue side down and the paper side up.
6. Cover with baking parchment.
7. Iron over the layers to melt the fusible glue and bond the Crash to the webbing.
8. Remove the baking parchment and place the Crash with the webbing to one side.

9. Tear the other piece of Crash into irregular shaped pieces. (Cutting with scissors will not leave the raggy edges required.)
10. Place the other piece of Crash onto the baking parchment.
11. Remove the backing paper from the Bondaweb.
12. Position the irregular shaped pieces over the glue side of the webbing.
13. Cover with baking parchment.
14. Iron to bond the pieces. If you have any pieces sticking up you should tear Bondaweb and patch it up by ironing over it.
15. Select the side that has the most texture and use this as the front of the fabric.
16. To colour the Crash you can use paints or dyes of your choice. The bags opposite were coloured with silk paints and encaustic wax.

Crash clutch bags

Fossil collection

Silk Paper Applique

The inspiration for this piece came from a seedpod found in a friend's garden a number of years ago. (Fig 1.)

1. I began by making two bonded layers of Crash as described on page 45.
2. Paint the re-formed Crash with gesso. I used white gesso but you can use black if desired. (Fig 2)
3. The background was coloured using pastel chalk crayons. (If you are using more expensive pastels you should wear a mask as they contain cadmium.)
4. It was sealed with gloss Mod Podge. When you paint over the chalky crayons they will smudge and merge to fill in any white areas. (Items opposite on page 47 were coloured in this way.)
5. Three silk paper shapes were cut out from left over scraps of red silk paper, which had been made previously.
6. Detached Buttonhole stitch was used to appliqué them to the re-formed Crash fabric.
7. The fabric was sealed again, using gloss Mod Podge.
8. Tim Holtz alcohol inks were used to add depth of colour and to integrate the piece.
9. Black Fuse FX was placed on top, covered with baking parchment and ironed in place.

Fig 1

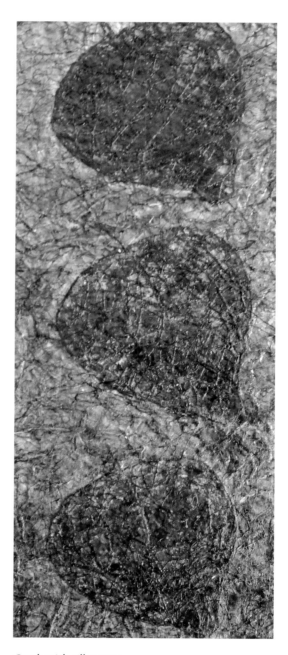

Fig 2

Crash with silk paper

Silk Scrim, Cocoon Strippings, Crash and Moulding Paste

This is a fragment from a large panel. The inspiration was old, worn fabric from a bygone age.

Fig 1

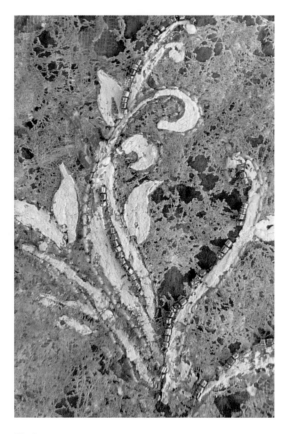

1. It consists of several layers. The first layer is a very tactile piece of silk gauze or scrim. (Scrim does not seem to describe this beautiful, appealing fabric.)
2. The second layer is cocoon strippings. These were ironed on in selected areas so that it looked patchy. Tease the strippings and place them randomly on the scrim. Spray with water. Cover with baking parchment and iron over the selected areas to temporarily bond them to the scrim.
3. The third layer is distressed Crash. One layer of Crash fabric was distressed using a heat tool.
4. The fourth layer is Golden's light moulding paste. This was applied sparingly so that it would appear to have worn away.
5. The first two layers were coloured with Brusho paints. Then the Crash was coloured with diluted silk paint.
6. The stencilled light moulding paste was coloured with layers of paint so that it appeared to be worn. The paints, which I selected to use, are the chalky acrylic paints by PaperArtsy called Fresco finish.
7. Embroidery ensures that all of the layers remain intact.

Fig 2

Layering and distressing fabrics

49

CHAPTER THREE

Unconventional Fabrics

"Medieval tiles"

Bubble Wrap

Try using bubble wrap as an alternative to batting. It quite surprisingly acts as a good substitute for some applications such as book covers. Working with bubble wrap can be an exhilarating experience. It can also be frustrating, as it does not receive all paints kindly. In this chapter I have experimented using a variety of colouring techniques.

BUBBLE WRAP AND GRATED WAX CRAYONS

My students have often heard me say that wax crayons are unsuitable for wearable art because they melt in the sun. I still do prefer to use encaustic wax for wearable art. If the cheaper alternative is to be used then ideally it should be sandwiched between layers, otherwise it could re-melt or flake off. There are a number of ways in which you can sandwich layers together. For this technique I have sandwiched bubble wrap, with grated crayons and inkjet printed teabag paper. You could use any thin paper such as bookbinders tissue instead of the teabag paper.

1. The work surface should be covered with newspapers to protect the area. Grating wax crayons can be a messy job. Grate a small amount of wax onto the bubble wrap. Use more than one colour and spread it around sparingly. When it is melted it will go a long way.
2. Place a second sheet of bubble wrap over the work.
3. Cover it with baking parchment.
4. With the iron set on low iron over the baking parchment. Take care not to get wax on the iron or alternatively use an encaustic iron.
5. I decided to seal my bubble wrap layers with inkjet printed teabag paper. I used Mod Podge sealer to do this. The paper is porous. Just place it on top and paint the sealer over it.
6. Black weed suppressant was used as a stabiliser on the back.

Bag and book cover made from bubble wrap

Encaustic Wax On Bubblewrap

I found that children's wax crayons were messy to work with and I much prefer working with encaustic wax. You use very little for this technique.

1. To work with encaustic wax, begin by melting the wax onto a flat iron. Iron this onto baking parchment. (Irons should always be set on low so that you do not breathe in any fumes.)
2. Turn the waxed parchment over the bubble wrap.
3. Cover with clean baking parchment.
4. Iron over the top to re-melt the wax. The wax will be transferred onto the bubble wrap.

MAKING HOLES IN THE BUBBLE WRAP

Once you have coloured the bubble wrap with coloured wax you may want to make holes through the layers so that you can layer the bubble wrap onto a second fabric. You could use an awl or a large needle to do this. You could also use a hole punch to punch out the holes.

Eileen Walls uses a soldering iron to make holes in waxed bubble wrap.

I am quite sure that for this technique you will need to use a respirator and mask. Do take care when burning plastics. I personally would only do this technique outside and whilst wearing a mask and respirator. If in doubt about burning plastic and wax then play safe. – Do this at your own risk.

1. Colour the bubble wrap with wax, as already explained.
2. Burn through each bubble with a hot soldering iron being careful to leave the spaces between the bubbles intact. Do this by holding the bubble wrap in mid air with one hand and poking the soldering iron through the bubbles. – Watch the fingers though!
3. Cut a piece of backing fabric. Make it a bit larger than the waxed bubble wrap.
4. Pin the bubble wrap on top of the fabric with a few safety pins - just sufficient to hold the two together.
5. Set the sewing machine to do free machining and stitch in circles around each hole in the bubble wrap.

Eileen Walls

Covering Waxed Bubble Wrap
With Dyed Scrim

Consider altering waxed bubble wrap by covering it with distressed dyed scrim. Large bubbles in the waxed wrap were used to make the fabric illustrated below.

1. Begin by using encaustic wax and ironing it onto the bubble wrap.

2. Pin together layers of fabric, starting with black weed suppressant on the bottom, then the waxed bubble wrap and finally, dyed scrim.
3. Use free machine embroidery to stitch into the layers.
4. Add hand stitching and beading if desired.

Weed suppressant, bubble wrap and scrim

Bubble Wrap Patterns

If you iron encaustic wax onto baking parchment and then iron it onto bubble wrap you will colour the bubble wrap but you will also obtain a pattern on the baking parchment.

You can then use this pattern and iron it onto other fabrics-thus obtaining two for the price of one.

Fig 1

Work like this:

1. Select the encaustic wax in your chosen colours. Melt the wax on the iron and iron it onto baking parchment.
2. Turn the baking parchment over and place it face down on the bubble wrap.
3. Iron over the parchment to transfer the wax. (Fig 1)

4. You will find that the bubble wrap will get coloured. At the same time some of the wax will remain on the parchment but it will have taken on the circular pattern of the bubble wrap. (Fig 2)

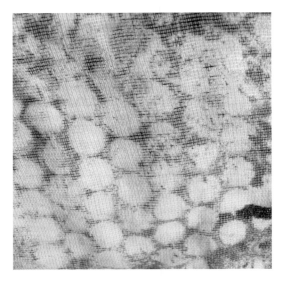

Fig 3

5. You can re-use this waxed pattern for another project. Turn the waxed side over, face down onto fabric of your choice. (I chose Azeta fabric.)
6. Iron it again and the pattern will be transferred to the fabric. (Fig 3)

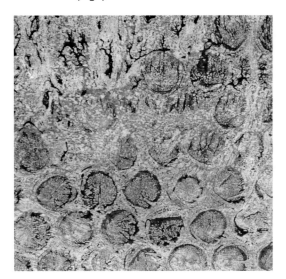

Fig 2

Detail of Azeta on the vessel

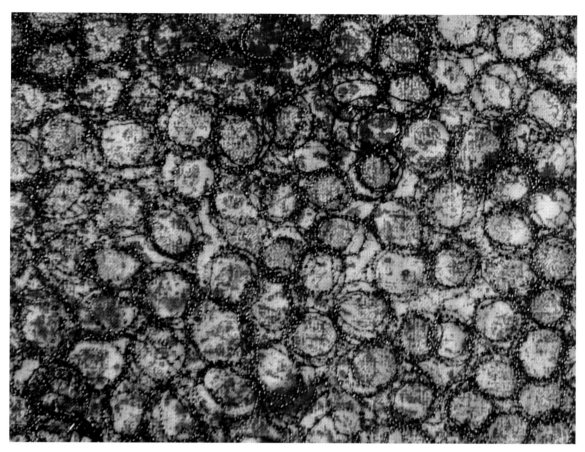

Azeta fabric, waxed and stitched

Azeta fabric with vegetarian silk lining and szerkezet rim

Peelable Glass Paints

The glass paints, which I have used here are those which are intended to stick on window panes. You work first with an outliner on baking Teflon and when that is dry you block in the rest of the colour. When it is dry (normally 24 hours) you can peel it off and it will automatically adhere to a glass windowpane. It peels off easily and does not leave a mess. It does however easily stick to itself so care should be taken to ensure that you do not fold it to itself. You can work with this paint in a number of ways.

I used a stamped image for the design on this bag. The quilted affect on this bag was achieved by layering bubble wrap with printed cotton fabric and cotton wadding, otherwise known as batting.

1. Use a bought stamp or make your own. I found that spongy stamps work well on the bubble wrap. Rubber stamps or wooden stamps with great detail are not so effective. If you cannot find an appropriate foam stamp consider making your own from Funky Foam.
2. Paint the glass paint onto the stamp and use the stamp on the bubble wrap. If you accidentally smudge the paint use a wet baby wipe to remove it all and start again.

3. Leave it to dry. When it is dry you can colour the background. Use a second colour and paint the background with the glass paint.
4. Alternatively you could use alcohol inks to colour the background and also the stamped image at the same time.
5. Seal the paint by painting matt Mod Podge over the bubble wrap.

Bubble wrap and peelable glass paint
Background painted with alcohol ink.

Tags and Handles

Tags play an important part in bag design. They help to personalise your bag. The lining for this bag is bought fabric with ancient script printed on it. The tag echoes this design. It is made from inkjet printed waxed cocoon stripping paper.

If you do not want to use inkjet printing there are lots of rubber stamps with ancient script, which could be used instead. Clear encaustic wax was ironed over the printed script. It was then embroidered. Two pieces were made and placed back to back. They were joined by blanket stitch used round the edges.

The handles are made from wooden beads, rescued from an old car seat covering. They are threaded through leather thongs.

Peelable Glass Paints

Peelable glass paints tend to stick together so you should take this into consideration when working with them.

Not all paints will work successfully on bubble wrap. Experiment to see which you prefer.

For this panel I worked with Stewart Gill Byzantia and peelable glass paint. I sealed the top with Mod Podge. It still remains tacky and care should be taken to ensure that it does not stick to other surfaces.

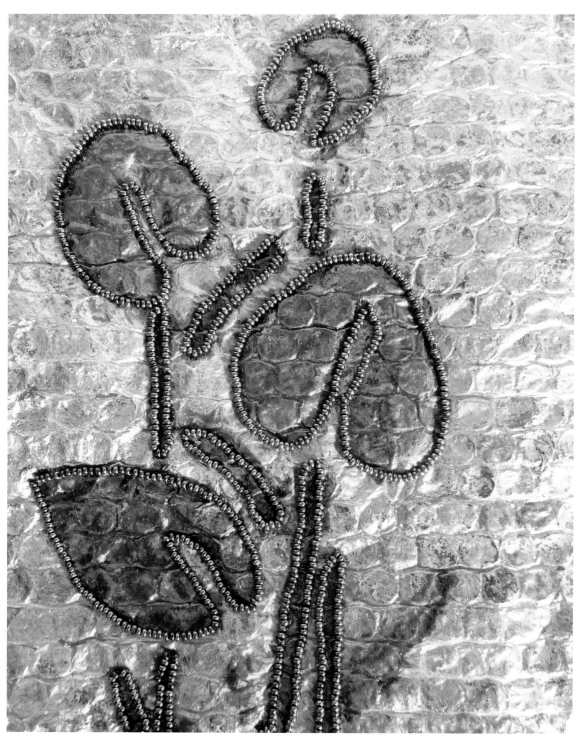

Waxed kozo paper and glass paints

Peelable Paints on Waxed Paper

For the book cover illustrated below I used textured kozo paper that had been used to clean wax on an encaustic iron. When the paper was saturated with wax and outlived its purpose, it was used for another project-and this is it.

Paint all over the paper. You can paint on the front or you can saturate the back and let the paint seep through. I use baby wipes to blend colours.
Use peelable glass paints to decorate designated areas.

The image opposite is a bought outline, sold for use with glass paints. I worked on top of foil, obtained from a used ground coffee bag. These glass paints stick well to this type of food bag foil.

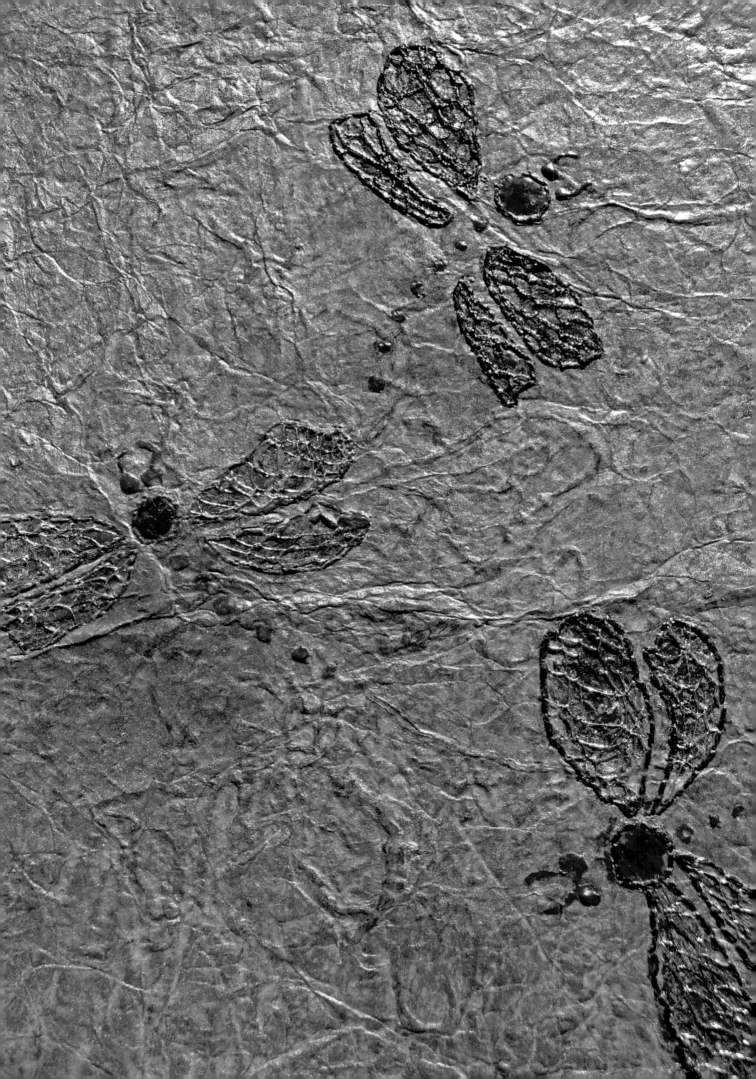

Glass Paint on Waxed Papers

This book cover was made using textured kozo paper. Whenever I am working with encaustic wax I clean the iron on textured kozo paper. When the paper is covered with wax it can be re-used. The colour of the wax does not matter. Whenever I work with gold bronzing powder mixed with acrylic wax I use any left overs on the papers which I have used to clean the iron. So this project was a freebie for me.

If you are starting from scratch, work like this;

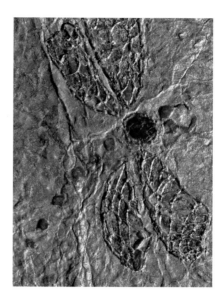

1. Iron encaustic wax onto textured kozo paper.
2. When you have ironed and covered the paper with wax then you can go on to paint it. Thin paints will not cover the wax. Thick paints will cover the wax but unless they are transparent they could obliterate the shades of wax. Try mixing gold bronzing powder with acrylic wax. Follow the safety recommendations when working with powders. I used this paint to paint over the wax.
3. When it is dry, paint your chosen design on the paper. My dragonflies were painted with encaustic wax using an encaustic stylus. But you could use a dedicated paintbrush. Melt the wax on an iron and paint it on the paper.
4. Rub clear beeswax polish into the paper. Rub with clean paper towels until it dries. As you rub and create a bloom you will see that the underlying encaustic wax will begin to shine through.
5. Embroider your design.
6. Use clear peelable glass paint to paint the dragonfly wings. As an alternative you could use a varnish or a clear glaze.

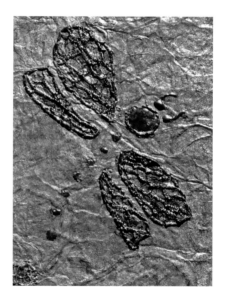

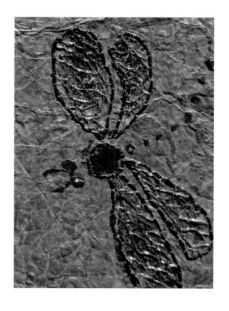

Waxed kozo paper and glass paints

Weed Suppressant and Flour Paste

Rather than using mediums such as InkAid or Digital Ground to cover the fabric try painting a thick solution of flour and water paste over weed suppressant. Work on baking parchment because the weed suppressant is porous. When it is dry cut the fabric to A4 size. Protect the edges using masking tape and inkjet print onto it. You may need to use a carrier sheet, depending on your printer.

Alternatively you can paint or stamp onto the weed suppressant after it has been painted with the flour and water paste.

Medieval tile

Weed Suppressant and Book Binders Tisssue

Try bonding coloured tissue to the weed suppressant. In the example below blue abaca tissue was bonded to the weed suppressant. To do this the tissue was placed over the suppressant and it was painted with matt Mod Podge.

When it is dry you can decorate the paper. This bag was painted with peelable glass paint.

Computer Paper

Computer paper can be transformed by painting glass paints on it.

Work like this:

1. Draw your design onto the paper.
2. Use a paintbrush or the nozzle on the paints to apply the colour. You may need to wait until each area is set before proceeding with the adjacent colour.
3. Two coats may be necessary and you should wait until each layer is dry before applying the next.
4. When it is dry you can stitch into the paper. I did not use a stabiliser because it would have made the paper too thick for my requirements.
5. Use as desired. I wanted a jazzy bangle. Copydex glue was used to bond the paper to the brass bangle blank.

Computer paper jewellery

Fish Scales

Do not overlook the attraction of fish scale beads. Fish scale beads are better than they sound. They do not smell! At least, that is to say, they do smell initially but once treated they are fine. To treat them simply wash them in soap and water a few times and rinse them a few times. Leave them to dry. Whilst they are wet you can bend them and curl them in position if desired.

Embroiderers in the past have used them to great effect.

I have used fish scales as beads on a number of projects. You can paint them with whatever you like. You can leave them matt or you can varnish them.

Obviously the size of the fish scale bead will be dependant on the size of the fish.

You can attach them to your artwork by sewing with a needle- no need to punch holes.

Large or small they can be great fun to work with.

Fish scale beads on painted squares

Working with Baby Wipes

It is amazing the difference you will find if you paint with wet baby wipes (wet wipes) as opposed to using a paintbrush. As this is a messy operation you should therefore protect your hands by wearing latex gloves. Merging colours can be an exciting adventure when using wet baby wipes to blend colours. The technique takes a little practice and the results will vary according to your surfaces. The main thing is not to be afraid. Dip the wet baby wipe directly into the paint. Dip into another colour and apply. If you do not like the results, take a second baby wipe and wipe the fabric.

PAINTING ON THE BACK OF FABRICS AND PAPERS

Merging colours works particularly well if you use a baby wipe and paint to colour the back of a piece of work. The colours seep through the fabric or paper, depending upon how absorbent the fabric is. I particularly like to use this technique if a resist has been applied to the front of the artwork.

Do not throw the used baby wipes away. Spread them on baking parchment and leave them to dry. When they are dry you can use them as fabric.

Baby wipes are stretchy and because of this they stretch around a mould for vessel making. They can be used in conjunction with other fabrics. Scrim was used with a painted baby wipe for this vessel illustrated below.

You are of course limited by size when working with baby wipes. Because they are stretchy you can pull and manipulate them. Some makes are bigger than others. You will find that they only stretch in one direction. Consider using them for patchwork.

I used two baby wipes for the A5 book illustrated. You can leave an open spine or you can make fabric to act as a decorative spine. The fish cookery book illustrated below was first painted blue. The fish were stencilled onto the baby wipe using light moulding paste.

As the paste was applied sparingly the original colour on the baby wipe bled and coloured the paste. White Misty Fuse was ironed over the top and a homemade stamp depicting wavy weeds was used over the whole piece. Although it is not obvious, stamping over the whole fabric in this way helped to add interest and integrated the fish.

Fish cookery book

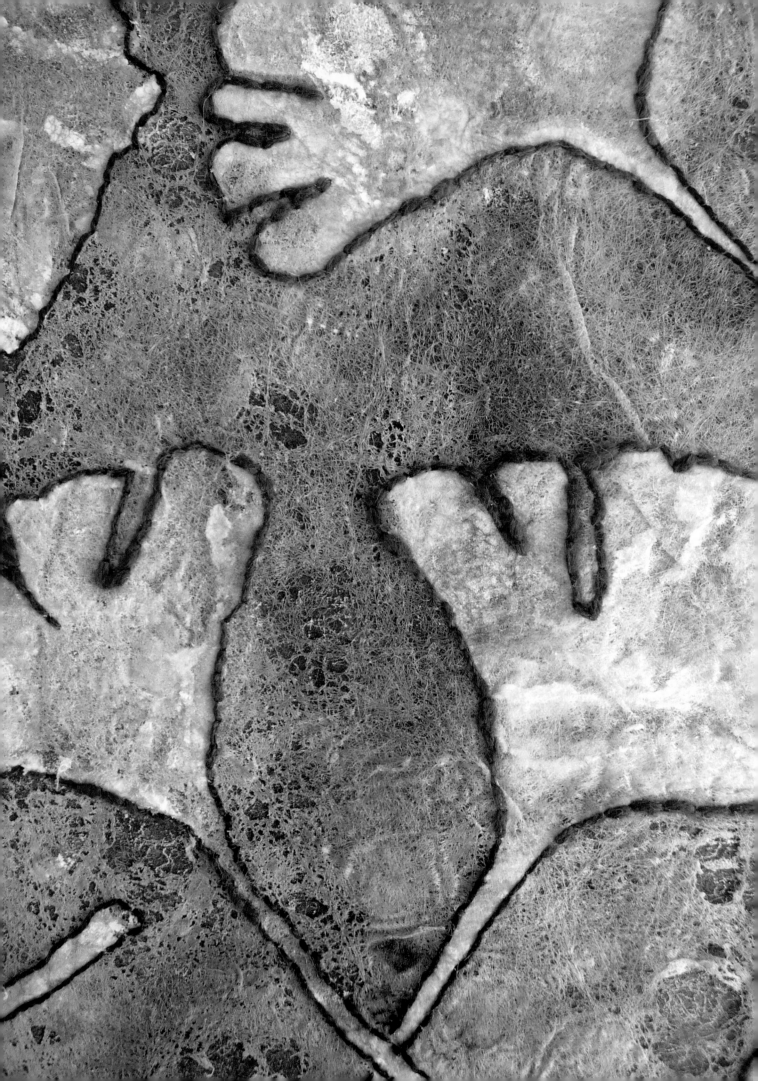

Baby Wipes with Crash

This fabric was made using two baby wipes, which had dark blue paint on them. When using the wipes as a painting tool it is worth considering deliberately using more than one so that you have matching colours to work with afterwards. It is really annoying if you only colour one wipe and then afterwards have to try to replicate another to match the first one.

YOU WILL NEED:

- Two coloured wet wipes
- Baking parchment
- 2 pieces of Crash, slightly larger than the wet wipes
- Paints of your choice (I used silk paints.)
- Paste
- Stencil
- Fuse FX or Mistyfuse

Method:

1. Colour two wet wipes or use two that have been used to colour other fabrics.
2. Spread them out to dry on baking parchment.
3. Distress two pieces of Crash fabric with a heat tool.
4. Colour the Crash. I used silk paints to do this. I ran the Crash under a tap to soak it prior to painting with the blue paint. This ensured that the colour was not too intense.
5. Place a stencil on the dry baby wipe. Push and scrape light moulding paste by Golden sparingly through the stencil.
6. I wanted the dark blue paint on the baby wipe to show through. Because the paint on the baby wipe had not been fixed it seeped through the moulding paste to give it a hint of blue.
7. When the paste is dry, cover the baby wipe with fusible webbing such as white Fuse FX or Mistyfuse.
8. Place the distressed Crash fabric over the top.
9. Cover these layers with baking parchment and iron over the top to fuse the layers.
10. Sometimes it is desirable to place a second layer of fusible webbing over the top. If you iron for prolonged periods with a hot iron the webbing sinks into the fabrics. The point of using this webbing is so that it can be seen so you may have to rectify this by ironing on a second layer.
11. You can stitch into the layers. I did not use a stabiliser, as I wanted thin fabric for the book covers. You could bond the wet wipe to a stabiliser of your choice. Cotton batting is, of course, excellent if you want a quilted effect. I use 505-spray glue to bond fabrics to stabilisers. This repositionable glue remains easy to stitch into. If you select to use an iron on stabiliser be aware that the Crash fabric responds to heat, as does the fusible webbing.

Baby wipe, Crash, and light moulding paste

Thick Flour Paste

Thick flour and water pastes are an economical way of obtaining a crackle finish. Sadly this paste has a tendency to crack, whether you want it to or not but you can make use of this. Knowing that it will not be as stable as some bought crackle paints, it will be necessary to seal it with a strong sealer such as Mod Podge.

To make the book cover illustrated below I worked like this:

1. Make cocoon stripping paper as described on page 75.
2. Mix flour and water to make a stiff paste, without any lumps.
3. Place a stencil over the paper and use a spatula or used credit card to push the thick paste over the stencil. Remove the stencil carefully.
4. When the paste is dry the paper and the paste can be coloured with paints of your choice.
5. When this is dry the paper and the stencil should be sealed. I used Mod Podge.

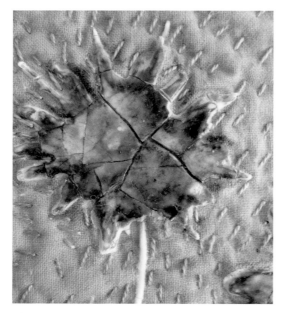

Flour paste stencilled on calico

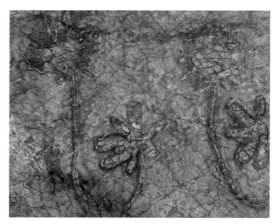

Flour paste stencilled on dyed baby wipe

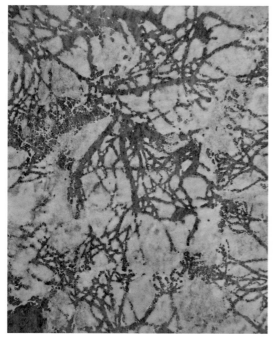

Flour paste stencilled on dyed batting

Flour paste stencilled on dyed baby wipe

Dyed Batting

Left over pieces of batting are very useful for a number of things. I use cotton batting to apply alcohol inks to shiny fabrics or papers. Wool batting is great if it is dyed. I used silk dye to colour the left over batting for this bag.

The inspiration for this "stone" bag came from a fabulous rock pool seen in Minnie Water, Australia. The rocks were the most amazing colour.

Little lightweight stones were collected and dyed to represent the colours observed in the rock pool on the beach. The pebbles on the dyed batting are made from light moulding paste. Black fusible webbing was ironed over the fabric to represent veins in the pebbles.

"Minnie Water-Rock pool"

CHAPTER FOUR

More Mixed Media Techniques

DRAWING WITH AN ENCAUSTIC STYLUS

My latest "toy" is a wonderful tool for drawing with wax. The encaustic art stylus, very cleverly, sucks up encaustic wax from the coloured wax block, and retains it in the nib until it comes into contact with the fabric that you are working on.

The bookmark and book covers, illustrated were worked on habotai silk.

1. Place the silk on baking parchment. The silk will be porous and any mixed media will soak through to the other side. By placing it on baking parchment it will be easier to remove afterwards.
2. Dip the stylus into the wax block. Do not push. The heat on the stylus will melt the wax and the wax will be drawn into the recess. It will remain there until it comes into contact with your fabric. You can draw shapes of your choice and fill them in with wax. Or you can draw outlines and use the wax as a resist and colour the designated areas with silk dyes.
3. If you wish, you can paint acrylic wax in designated areas, sprinkle embossing powder over the wet acrylic wax and heat with a heat tool to melt the powder. The red area on the bookmark was embellished with red enamelling powder. The same red enamelling powder was used over red silk paper to make the tapes for the book with the open spine (Below, opposite)
4. If you seal the fabric with acrylic wax it will intensify the colour. The bookmark opposite, left, was sealed with acrylic wax and beeswax polish.

Silk book covers with encaustic wax applied in selected areas using an encaustic stylus.
Isobel Hall and Xantha Hall

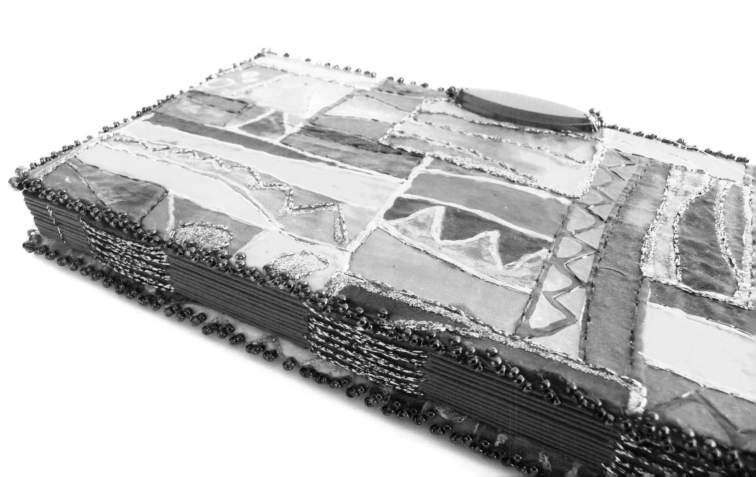

Medieval Inspired Books

I love to make these cocoon stripping books. To age the cocoon stripping pages I colour them with instant coffee. For a touch of opulence try ironing gold encaustic wax onto baking parchment and transfer it to the pages by placing it face down on the paper and ironing over it. Specks of black Fuse FX or Mistyfuse will also make a contribution to the ageing process. Wonderful caramelisation can be achieved by scorching the papers. (See strip above.) Use a hot iron to do this and keep the ironing moving over the baking parchment so that you do not end up with an iron mark! When working to make the diagonal lines, raggy tapes are a great help as these tend to give the illusion of an aged piece.

1. Begin by making the cocoon stripping paper. To do this tease the fibres out and place them on baking parchment. Spray cold water over them and cover with a second sheet of parchment. Iron with a hot iron. Build the layers up. (About 3 layers.)
2. Colour it with coffee and iron it dry between baking parchment. (Fig 1)
3. Use raggy edged tapes and sew them in a diagonal fashion. (Fig2)
4. Use an encaustic iron set on low to iron dark green encaustic wax in selected areas. (Dark blue would work as an alternative.)
5. Flood the paper and tapes with silver encaustic wax. (Fig 3)
6. Use alcohol inks and blending solution to add colour to the silver encaustic wax.

Fig 1

Fig 2

Fig 3

Make the pages and the covers from cocoon strippings. The pages can be coloured and embroidered prior to assembling them. Sandwich two completed layers together and stitch round the edges to make the pages.

OR:

Try colouring and embroidering the page. Turn it over and add a new layer of cocoon strippings. Spray cold water on the back and iron over baking parchment. To use this technique you must first check that the mixed media on the page will not be affected by water or heat.

Search for suitable accessories. For example old hinges can be further distressed as illustrated opposite. To do this, partially paint the metal, sand it back and then colour it with alcohol ink. Brads can be found in scrap booking shops. These can be re-coloured too.

Make embroidered spines using silk paper and attach this after using mixed media and embroidery.

Cocoon stripping paper books

Gesso Over Oil Paints

Gesso is used as an undercoat, to receive other mixed media. Good quality gesso will obliterate anything which is underneath. Cheaper makes may need two coats.

Try painting white gesso sparingly over other paints so that the bottom colours peep through but are not too obvious. I found that it works well over oil based colouring agents. The fresco opposite was first painted with oil paints on canvas. I worked like this:

1. Begin by painting the canvas or fabric of your choice. I used canvas, calico and Evolon fabric for my samples. Use oil paints or oil based crayons. Oil paints take longer to dry. Markal oil sticks take 24 hours. You can also use cheaper oil based crayons. The pattern is unimportant but you do need to cover all of the fabric.

2. When it is dry, paint the fabric with white gesso. Do not layer it on too thickly. You want to obliterate any design but have colour peeping through.

3. When this is dry select your images. Inkjet print the images onto thin paper such as bookbinders tissue or teabag paper. I chose images which were mainly black and white. Many of my photographs are from head stones in graveyards. (Top left) If you do not want to use a printer then you could use a stamp and inkpad. (Third down)

4. Laminate these to the fabric. To do this simply place them in position and paint over with a sealer. I used Mod Podge.

5. Colouring the background and the images is fun. Begin by colouring Bondaweb fusible webbing. You can paint with a paintbrush or use a spray paint, such as Brusho.

6. When the Bondaweb is dry, tear it into irregular shaped pieces. Place in position on the fabric. Cover with baking parchment and iron over it.

Sketchbook work

This sketchbook work is part of a study featuring distressed advertising billboards. Woven fabric was partially painted with gesso and light moulding paste. The architectural building is made from translucent liquid Sculpey. The transfer on this liquid polymer clay stands proud on the sketchbook page. As such it would be unsuitable for wearable art. To overcome this problem, but at the same time keep the image, the sketchbook work was photographed and inkjet printed onto thin paper. Different images were played with. I used teabag paper to print the images onto but bookbinders tissue could be used as a substitute.

The resulting bag illustrated below is a large shopping bag. (29cm x42cm excluding the handles.) It has been sealed with matt Mod Podge and is waterproof.

Shopping bag with billboard image and tickets, made using a Tim Holtz stamp

Working with Gesso

Medieval tiles fascinate me, especially if they are worn and have been exposed to the elements. The bag on the opposite page was made following a day out to study medieval tiles in ruined abbeys in North Yorkshire.

To make the fabric for this bag you can use up all of your scraps of fabrics. Combining textures and thickness is essential. I used anything from woven wool fabric, crocheted wool squares to silk and rayon fabrics. The colour at this stage does not matter too much as paint will be used in the latter stages.

PAINTING OVER STITCHES

1. Select your base fabric. I used cotton fabric, which already had tramlines sewn in a grid formation. To make your own use a sewing machine to sew tramlines in broad diagonal lines. They need to be about 5cm square and should be evenly spaced. These will represent the grout lines. You could use pin tucks to create a raised edge if desired.

2. Use free machine embroidery to add collaged pieces to each square. The motif should remain the same but scraps of fabrics of varying thickness should be incorporated. Stitch heavily round some of the motifs and lightly round others. Allow some of the fabric to "bubble". Leave some areas in the motif exposed and bare – likewise the surrounding area. You are creating texture, which will represent worn tiled ancient surfaces.

3. When the stitching has been completed, it is ready to paint.

4. Paint white gesso over the fabric, leaving some of the designated areas exposed.

5. When this is dry use heat fixable paint to colour the tiles. I used Stewart Gill heat fixable paint. Leave some areas so that the base colour shows through. This will represent worn patches.

6. Iron black fusible webbing over the fabric to heat fix the paints and at the same time to age it.

Bag representing a medieval tiled floor. Textured fabric tiles using scrap fabric

SUPPLIERS

UK

21ST century Yarns
Dyed scrim, felt, yarns
Unit 18, Langston Priory Workshops
Kingham
Oxon OX7 6UP
Yarns21stcentury@aol.com

Ario
Stewart Gill products, mixed media
5 Pengry Road
Loughor
Swansea SA4 6PH
fiona@ario.co.uk

Art Van Go
Fuse FX, mixed media
1 Stevenage Road
Knebworth
Herts SG3 6AN
art@artvango.co.uk

Barnyarns
Threads, sewing accessories
Canal Wharf
Bondgate Green
Ripon
North Yorks HG4 1AQ
www.barnyarns.co.uk

Colourcraft
Peelable glass paint, mixed media
Unit 6
555 Carlisle Street East
Sheffield
S4 8DT
www.colourcraft-ltd.com

Crafty Notions
Stencils, mixed media
Unit 2, Jessop Way
Newark NG24 2ER
www.craftynotions.com

L.B. Crafts
PaperArtsy paints
6 Rose Court
Market Place
Olney MK46 4BY
shop@lbcrafts.com

Gallery Textiles
Heat distressable paper
www.gallerytextiles.co.uk
sales@gallerytextiles.co.uk

Nid-noi.com
Crash, lutradur
126 Norwich Drive
Brighton BN2 4LL
info@nid-noi.com

Oliver Twists
Cocoon strippings, threads,silk fibres, dyed scrim
22 Phoenix Road
Crowther, Washington
Tyne and Wear NE38 0AD
olivertwistsretail@fsmail.net

Texere Yarns
Cocoon strippings, threads, silk fibres
College Road
Barkerend Road
Bradford BD1 4AV
info@texere.co.uk

Winifred Cottage
Vegetarian silk, szerkezet
17 Elms Road
Fleet
Hants GU51 3EG
sales@winifredcottage.co.uk

USA

Golden Artist Colors, Inc.
Golden products
188 Bell Road
New Berlin, NY 13411-9527
www.goldenpaints.com

Dick Blick Art Materials
Art supplies
PO Box 1267
Galesburg,IL 61402-1267
www.dickblick.com